Manifest the Man God Has for You

DAILY JOURNAL

STEPHAN LABOSSIERE

@stephanspeaks

Manifest the Man God Has for You Daily Journal
Copyright ©2019 by Stephan Labossiere for Stephan Speaks, LLC
Published by Highly Favored Publishing
First Edition: July 2019

For information, contact Highly Favored Publishing –
highlyfavoredent@gmail.com

Editor & Creative Consultant: C. Nzingha Smith
Formatting: Ya Ya Ya Creative – www.yayayacreative.com

ISBN No. 978-0-9980189-7-3

PRINTED AND BOUND IN THE UNITED STATES OF AMERICA

Introduction

Welcome to *Manifesting the Man God Has for You Daily Journal*. I'm glad you're here and ready to embark upon this new journey.

So many women desire to have an amazing relationship and the man of their dreams. However, because they've become jaded from dealing with so much nonsense, they often end up discouraged and damaged. The idea of ever meeting their dream guy seems unrealistic. I'm here to tell you, this doesn't have to be the case. I want to help you receive and experience the amazing relationship you desire.

The fact that you're embracing this path means you're still holding on to your hope. You are still believing, and you know deep inside that you can receive all that God has for you, including the man he created with you in mind.

This is the first step in the right direction. To get what we desire in life, we have to be willing to put in the work. We have to be willing to change our mindset and we have to be willing to be consistent with the proper effort to receive what we desire. This journal and the coaching program you are getting ready to begin is going to help you achieve just that.

By creating this journal, I wanted to give you a tool that's going to help move you in the right direction toward manifesting the man God has for you. It's going to allow you to mentally, spiritually, and emotionally focus. To get on the path you need to stay on to get results. It'll help keep you from getting distracted and discouraged while on your journey. It'll also help keep you from falling into the traps that so many women fall into that actually take them away from receiving what they truly desire.

This journal is my answer to God's call. This is me walking in my purpose. I've helped countless women achieve things they never thought they could. I have many clients that have gone from being single, frustrated, and ready to give up, to being engaged and married. They have gone on to be in great relationships. In the process, they've become happier and more fulfilled in life. I want to do the same for you.

Even though the focus of this journal is about manifesting the man God has for you, it's also about manifesting the great woman you are meant to be. It's about pulling out the positivity in you and helping you to dwell on thoughts and mindsets that are going to produce results for you. It's about reversing the negative mindsets that take you away from what you desire.

How Does the Manifest the Man God Has for You Journal Work?

Manifesting the Man God Has for You Daily Journal is a *daily tool to help you* clearly identify what you want in a man AND help you to develop the right mindset to attract this person into your life - in just 5 minutes a day. Simply follow the prompts in the journal every single day and you'll begin manifesting what you desire in your life.

STEP 1

Ground yourself in a daily affirmation. In this journal you will create the affirmation that's going to get you feeling good about yourself and starting your day with a positive attitude…which is very attractive to men by the way. Here are a few examples to give you ideas about what you can create as you prepare to write your own affirmations each day: "I am worthy of everything I desire in my life." "I am beautiful just as I am."

STEP 2

Recognize the blessings already in your life. This puts you into a gratitude state so that you can begin to develop the habit of being a person with positive energy. Now here's the thing about being a person with positive energy…it gets you noticed everywhere you go. It gets you attracting new men into your life because they want to get close to your great positive energy.

STEP 3

Take time daily to get clear with yourself on what kind of relationship you desire. This is how you set your own dating guidelines. Then you'll remind yourself of your dating guidelines every day, so you don't end up settling for less than what you deserve.

STEP 4

Request your godly man in prayer BOTH by praying to God and writing your prayer out in your Manifest Journal. Why is this so important? Because God told us to ask and we shall receive, therefore you need to make your request heard. Being specific with your prayer to get God working on your side, to bring into your life what you desire. In this case it's the man He wants you to be with.

The last step is the one that seals the deal. It's the most important step of all, though without the other steps, it's completely pointless.

STEP 5

Thank God for your man as if it's already been done. This gets you showing up in the world in your day-to-day life as if the relationship you desire already exists, so you become a vibrational match for what it is you are wanting to manifest and attract, and then it eventually does exist.

I really want you to enjoy this journey. I want you to embrace all that needs to be done and I want you to be patient. Listen, everything is not going to happen tomorrow or next week. I can say that if you stick with it, you're going to get what you desire. The man God has for you will be manifested. Even better than that. You're going to be so much better prepared and ready to receive him when he comes. Ready? Let's get started!

A woman who walks in her purpose doesn't have to chase people or opportunities. Her light causes people and opportunities to pursue her.

Today's Affirmation: _____

I am BLESSED with:

1. _____

2. _____

3. _____

4. _____

5. _____

MANIFEST THE MAN GOD HAS FOR YOU - DAILY PRACTICE

STEP 1: Get clear with yourself on what kind of relationship you desire. (First write it, then speak it.)

_____

_____

_____

_____

_____

STEP 2: Request it in prayer. (First write it, then speak it.)

_____

_____

_____

_____

_____

_____

_____

STEP 3: Thank God for it as if it's already been done. (First write it, then speak it.)

_____

_____

_____

_____

_____

_____

_____

_____

Always be the good woman that you are.
Just learn the difference between who is worth your time,
and those who don't deserve a second of it.

Today's Affirmation: _____

I am BLESSED with:

1. _____

2. _____

3. _____

4. _____

5. _____

MANIFEST THE MAN GOD HAS FOR YOU - DAILY PRACTICE

STEP 1: Get clear with yourself on what kind of relationship you desire. (First write it, then speak it.)

_____

_____

_____

_____

_____

STEP 2: Request it in prayer. (First write it, then speak it.)

_____

_____

_____

_____

_____

_____

_____

STEP 3: Thank God for it as if it's already been done. (First write it, then speak it.)

_____

_____

_____

_____

_____

_____

_____

_____

The man for you will be willing to listen to you, not dismiss how you feel.

Today's Affirmation: _____

I am BLESSED with:

1. _____

2. _____

3. _____

4. _____

5. _____

MANIFEST THE MAN GOD HAS FOR YOU - DAILY PRACTICE

STEP 1: Get clear with yourself on what kind of relationship you desire. (First write it, then speak it.)

_____

_____

_____

_____

_____

_____

STEP 2: Request it in prayer. (First write it, then speak it.)

_____

_____

_____

_____

_____

_____

_____

_____

STEP 3: Thank God for it as if it's already been done. (First write it, then speak it.)

_____

_____

_____

_____

_____

_____

_____

_____

The man God has for you wants to lead you with love and be the man that you can depend on.

Today's Affirmation: _____

I am BLESSED with:

1. _____

2. _____

3. _____

4. _____

5. _____

MANIFEST THE MAN GOD HAS FOR YOU - DAILY PRACTICE

STEP 1: Get clear with yourself on what kind of relationship you desire. (First write it, then speak it.)

_____

_____

_____

_____

_____

_____

STEP 2: Request it in prayer. (First write it, then speak it.)

_____

_____

_____

_____

_____

_____

_____

STEP 3: Thank God for it as if it's already been done. (First write it, then speak it.)

_____

_____

_____

_____

_____

_____

_____

Don't stress yourself out over a man that won't do right by you. You deserve better than that.

Today's Affirmation: _____

I am BLESSED with:

1. _____

2. _____

3. _____

4. _____

5. _____

MANIFEST THE MAN GOD HAS FOR YOU - DAILY PRACTICE

STEP 1: Get clear with yourself on what kind of relationship you desire. (First write it, then speak it.)

_____

_____

_____

_____

_____

_____

STEP 2: Request it in prayer. (First write it, then speak it.)

_____

_____

_____

_____

_____

_____

_____

STEP 3: Thank God for it as if it's already been done. (First write it, then speak it.)

_____

_____

_____

_____

_____

_____

_____

_____

If he pulls you away from God, then he's not the person God wants you to be with.

Today's Affirmation: _____

I am BLESSED with:

1. _____

2. _____

3. _____

4. _____

5. _____

MANIFEST THE MAN GOD HAS FOR YOU - DAILY PRACTICE

STEP 1: Get clear with yourself on what kind of relationship you desire. (First write it, then speak it.)

_____

_____

_____

_____

_____

_____

STEP 2: Request it in prayer. (First write it, then speak it.)

_____

_____

_____

_____

_____

_____

_____

STEP 3: Thank God for it as if it's already been done. (First write it, then speak it.)

_____

_____

_____

_____

_____

_____

_____

_____

Boys will bring you confusion & chaos.
Men desire to provide you with clarity & peace.

Today's Affirmation: _____

I am BLESSED with:

1. _____

2. _____

3. _____

4. _____

5. _____

MANIFEST THE MAN GOD HAS FOR YOU - DAILY PRACTICE

STEP 1: Get clear with yourself on what kind of relationship you desire. (First write it, then speak it.)

_____

_____

_____

_____

_____

_____

STEP 2: Request it in prayer. (First write it, then speak it.)

_____

_____

_____

_____

_____

_____

_____

_____

STEP 3: Thank God for it as if it's already been done. (First write it, then speak it.)

_____

_____

_____

_____

_____

_____

_____

_____

Who you want isn't always who is best for you.

Today's Affirmation: _____

I am BLESSED with:

1. _____

2. _____

3. _____

4. _____

5. _____

MANIFEST THE MAN GOD HAS FOR YOU - DAILY PRACTICE

STEP 1: Get clear with yourself on what kind of relationship you desire. (First write it, then speak it.)

_____

_____

_____

_____

_____

_____

STEP 2: Request it in prayer. (First write it, then speak it.)

_____

_____

_____

_____

_____

_____

_____

_____

STEP 3: Thank God for it as if it's already been done. (First write it, then speak it.)

_____

_____

_____

_____

_____

_____

_____

_____

Don't date his potential, date his reality.

Today's Affirmation: _____

I am BLESSED with:

1. _____

2. _____

3. _____

4. _____

5. _____

MANIFEST THE MAN GOD HAS FOR YOU - DAILY PRACTICE

STEP 1: Get clear with yourself on what kind of relationship you desire. (First write it, then speak it.)

_____

_____

_____

_____

_____

_____

STEP 2: Request it in prayer. (First write it, then speak it.)

_____

_____

_____

_____

_____

_____

_____

STEP 3: Thank God for it as if it's already been done. (First write it, then speak it.)

_____

_____

_____

_____

_____

_____

_____

_____

When you know deep inside, he isn't the man for you, stop giving him opportunities to waste your time.

Today's Affirmation: _____

I am BLESSED with:

1. _____

2. _____

3. _____

4. _____

5. _____

MANIFEST THE MAN GOD HAS FOR YOU - DAILY PRACTICE

STEP 1: Get clear with yourself on what kind of relationship you desire. (First write it, then speak it.)

_____

_____

_____

_____

_____

_____

STEP 2: Request it in prayer. (First write it, then speak it.)

_____

_____

_____

_____

_____

_____

_____

_____

STEP 3: Thank God for it as if it's already been done. (First write it, then speak it.)

_____

_____

_____

_____

_____

_____

_____

_____

*If you truly want a good man,
then stop entertaining a bad one.*

Today's Affirmation: _____

I am BLESSED with:

1. _____

2. _____

3. _____

4. _____

5. _____

MANIFEST THE MAN GOD HAS FOR YOU - DAILY PRACTICE

STEP 1: Get clear with yourself on what kind of relationship you desire. (First write it, then speak it.)

_____

_____

_____

_____

_____

_____

STEP 2: Request it in prayer. (First write it, then speak it.)

_____

_____

_____

_____

_____

_____

_____

STEP 3: Thank God for it as if it's already been done. (First write it, then speak it.)

_____

_____

_____

_____

_____

_____

_____

_____

*A good woman doesn't lower her standards.
She knows what she deserves and doesn't settle for less.*

Today's Affirmation: _____

I am BLESSED with:

1. _____

2. _____

3. _____

4. _____

5. _____

MANIFEST THE MAN GOD HAS FOR YOU - DAILY PRACTICE

STEP 1: Get clear with yourself on what kind of relationship you desire. (First write it, then speak it.)

_____

_____

_____

_____

_____

_____

STEP 2: Request it in prayer. (First write it, then speak it.)

_____

_____

_____

_____

_____

_____

_____

_____

STEP 3: Thank God for it as if it's already been done. (First write it, then speak it.)

_____

_____

_____

_____

_____

_____

_____

_____

You are blessed.

Today's Affirmation: _____

I am BLESSED with:

1. _____

2. _____

3. _____

4. _____

5. _____

MANIFEST THE MAN GOD HAS FOR YOU - DAILY PRACTICE

STEP 1: Get clear with yourself on what kind of relationship you desire. (First write it, then speak it.)

_____

_____

_____

_____

_____

_____

STEP 2: Request it in prayer. (First write it, then speak it.)

_____

_____

_____

_____

_____

_____

_____

_____

STEP 3: Thank God for it as if it's already been done. (First write it, then speak it.)

_____

_____

_____

_____

_____

_____

_____

_____

You deserve a man who is ready to give you the commitment you desire.

Today's Affirmation: _____

I am BLESSED with:

1. _____

2. _____

3. _____

4. _____

5. _____

MANIFEST THE MAN GOD HAS FOR YOU - DAILY PRACTICE

STEP 1: Get clear with yourself on what kind of relationship you desire. (First write it, then speak it.)

_____

_____

_____

_____

_____

_____

STEP 2: Request it in prayer. (First write it, then speak it.)

_____

_____

_____

_____

_____

_____

_____

STEP 3: Thank God for it as if it's already been done. (First write it, then speak it.)

_____

_____

_____

_____

_____

_____

_____

Don't push a great man away because the hurt from your past makes you constantly question his love.

Today's Affirmation: _____

I am BLESSED with:

1. _____

2. _____

3. _____

4. _____

5. _____

MANIFEST THE MAN GOD HAS FOR YOU - DAILY PRACTICE

STEP 1: Get clear with yourself on what kind of relationship you desire. (First write it, then speak it.)

_____

_____

_____

_____

_____

_____

STEP 2: Request it in prayer. (First write it, then speak it.)

_____

_____

_____

_____

_____

_____

_____

STEP 3: Thank God for it as if it's already been done. (First write it, then speak it.)

_____

_____

_____

_____

_____

_____

_____

Be with someone who wants to pursue God with you.

Today's Affirmation: _____

I am BLESSED with:

1. _____

2. _____

3. _____

4. _____

5. _____

MANIFEST THE MAN GOD HAS FOR YOU - DAILY PRACTICE

STEP 1: Get clear with yourself on what kind of relationship you desire. (First write it, then speak it.)

_____

_____

_____

_____

_____

_____

STEP 2: Request it in prayer. (First write it, then speak it.)

_____

_____

_____

_____

_____

_____

_____

STEP 3: Thank God for it as if it's already been done. (First write it, then speak it.)

_____

_____

_____

_____

_____

_____

_____

_____

If you love them, pray for them.

Today's Affirmation: _____

I am BLESSED with:

1. _____

2. _____

3. _____

4. _____

5. _____

MANIFEST THE MAN GOD HAS FOR YOU - DAILY PRACTICE

STEP 1: Get clear with yourself on what kind of relationship you desire. (First write it, then speak it.)

_____

_____

_____

_____

_____

_____

STEP 2: Request it in prayer. (First write it, then speak it.)

_____

_____

_____

_____

_____

_____

_____

_____

STEP 3: Thank God for it as if it's already been done. (First write it, then speak it.)

_____

_____

_____

_____

_____

_____

_____

_____

You run a lot of risks trying to be in a relationship with a man's "potential".

Today's Affirmation: _____

I am BLESSED with:

1. _____

2. _____

3. _____

4. _____

5. _____

MANIFEST THE MAN GOD HAS FOR YOU - DAILY PRACTICE

STEP 1: Get clear with yourself on what kind of relationship you desire. (First write it, then speak it.)

_____

_____

_____

_____

_____

_____

STEP 2: Request it in prayer. (First write it, then speak it.)

_____

_____

_____

_____

_____

_____

_____

_____

STEP 3: Thank God for it as if it's already been done. (First write it, then speak it.)

_____

_____

_____

_____

_____

_____

_____

_____

The man God has for you will not abuse you or disrespect you. He will love you and cherish you.

Today's Affirmation: _____

I am BLESSED with:

1. _____

2. _____

3. _____

4. _____

5. _____

MANIFEST THE MAN GOD HAS FOR YOU - DAILY PRACTICE

STEP 1: Get clear with yourself on what kind of relationship you desire. (First write it, then speak it.)

_____

_____

_____

_____

_____

_____

STEP 2: Request it in prayer. (First write it, then speak it.)

_____

_____

_____

_____

_____

_____

_____

_____

STEP 3: Thank God for it as if it's already been done. (First write it, then speak it.)

_____

_____

_____

_____

_____

_____

_____

_____

Don't get so focused on him, that you
lose sight of what you need to do for you.

Today's Affirmation: _____

I am BLESSED with:

1. _____

2. _____

3. _____

4. _____

5. _____

MANIFEST THE MAN GOD HAS FOR YOU - DAILY PRACTICE

STEP 1: Get clear with yourself on what kind of relationship you desire. (First write it, then speak it.)

_____

_____

_____

_____

_____

_____

STEP 2: Request it in prayer. (First write it, then speak it.)

_____

_____

_____

_____

_____

_____

_____

STEP 3: Thank God for it as if it's already been done. (First write it, then speak it.)

_____

_____

_____

_____

_____

_____

_____

*If they're serious about you,
then their words and actions will be consistent.*

Today's Affirmation: _____

I am BLESSED with:

1. _____

2. _____

3. _____

4. _____

5. _____

MANIFEST THE MAN GOD HAS FOR YOU - DAILY PRACTICE

STEP 1: Get clear with yourself on what kind of relationship you desire. (First write it, then speak it.)

_____

_____

_____

_____

_____

_____

STEP 2: Request it in prayer. (First write it, then speak it.)

_____

_____

_____

_____

_____

_____

_____

STEP 3: Thank God for it as if it's already been done. (First write it, then speak it.)

_____

_____

_____

_____

_____

_____

_____

You deserve a man who loves you, respects you, and is attentive to your needs. Don't feel like you have to settle for anything less.

Today's Affirmation: _____

I am BLESSED with:

1. _____

2. _____

3. _____

4. _____

5. _____

MANIFEST THE MAN GOD HAS FOR YOU - DAILY PRACTICE

STEP 1: Get clear with yourself on what kind of relationship you desire. (First write it, then speak it.)

_____

_____

_____

_____

_____

STEP 2: Request it in prayer. (First write it, then speak it.)

_____

_____

_____

_____

_____

_____

_____

_____

STEP 3: Thank God for it as if it's already been done. (First write it, then speak it.)

_____

_____

_____

_____

_____

_____

_____

_____

What's coming is better than what's gone.

Today's Affirmation: _____

I am BLESSED with:

1. _____

2. _____

3. _____

4. _____

5. _____

MANIFEST THE MAN GOD HAS FOR YOU - DAILY PRACTICE

STEP 1: Get clear with yourself on what kind of relationship you desire. (First write it, then speak it.)

_____

_____

_____

_____

_____

_____

STEP 2: Request it in prayer. (First write it, then speak it.)

_____

_____

_____

_____

_____

_____

_____

_____

STEP 3: Thank God for it as if it's already been done. (First write it, then speak it.)

_____

_____

_____

_____

_____

_____

_____

_____

You deserve the love you keep trying to give everyone else.

Today's Affirmation: _____

I am BLESSED with:

1. _____

2. _____

3. _____

4. _____

5. _____

MANIFEST THE MAN GOD HAS FOR YOU - DAILY PRACTICE

STEP 1: Get clear with yourself on what kind of relationship you desire. (First write it, then speak it.)

_____

_____

_____

_____

_____

_____

STEP 2: Request it in prayer. (First write it, then speak it.)

_____

_____

_____

_____

_____

_____

_____

_____

STEP 3: Thank God for it as if it's already been done. (First write it, then speak it.)

_____

_____

_____

_____

_____

_____

_____

_____

Trust God's timing.

Today's Affirmation: _____

I am BLESSED with:

1. _____

2. _____

3. _____

4. _____

5. _____

MANIFEST THE MAN GOD HAS FOR YOU - DAILY PRACTICE

STEP 1: Get clear with yourself on what kind of relationship you desire. (First write it, then speak it.)

_____

_____

_____

_____

_____

_____

STEP 2: Request it in prayer. (First write it, then speak it.)

_____

_____

_____

_____

_____

_____

_____

_____

STEP 3: Thank God for it as if it's already been done. (First write it, then speak it.)

_____

_____

_____

_____

_____

_____

_____

_____

*If he isn't going to be consistent, then you
no longer need to be present in his life.*

Today's Affirmation: _____

I am BLESSED with:

1. _____

2. _____

3. _____

4. _____

5. _____

MANIFEST THE MAN GOD HAS FOR YOU - DAILY PRACTICE

STEP 1: Get clear with yourself on what kind of relationship you desire. (First write it, then speak it.)

_____

_____

_____

_____

_____

_____

STEP 2: Request it in prayer. (First write it, then speak it.)

_____

_____

_____

_____

_____

_____

_____

STEP 3: Thank God for it as if it's already been done. (First write it, then speak it.)

_____

_____

_____

_____

_____

_____

_____

_____

There's a man out there searching for everything you're giving to a man who doesn't appreciate it.

Today's Affirmation: _____

I am BLESSED with:

1. _____

2. _____

3. _____

4. _____

5. _____

MANIFEST THE MAN GOD HAS FOR YOU - DAILY PRACTICE

STEP 1: Get clear with yourself on what kind of relationship you desire. (First write it, then speak it.)

_____

_____

_____

_____

_____

_____

STEP 2: Request it in prayer. (First write it, then speak it.)

_____

_____

_____

_____

_____

_____

_____

STEP 3: Thank God for it as if it's already been done. (First write it, then speak it.)

_____

_____

_____

_____

_____

_____

_____

*It's not about finding a man to complete you.
It's about completing yourself first,
and receiving the man who compliments you.*

Today's Affirmation: _____

I am BLESSED with:

1. _____

2. _____

3. _____

4. _____

5. _____

MANIFEST THE MAN GOD HAS FOR YOU - DAILY PRACTICE

STEP 1: Get clear with yourself on what kind of relationship you desire. (First write it, then speak it.)

_____

_____

_____

_____

_____

STEP 2: Request it in prayer. (First write it, then speak it.)

_____

_____

_____

_____

_____

_____

_____

_____

STEP 3: Thank God for it as if it's already been done. (First write it, then speak it.)

_____

_____

_____

_____

_____

_____

_____

_____

*You won't have to chase the man God has for you.
He'll know and embrace your worth.*

Today's Affirmation: _____

I am BLESSED with:

1. _____

2. _____

3. _____

4. _____

5. _____

MANIFEST THE MAN GOD HAS FOR YOU - DAILY PRACTICE

STEP 1: Get clear with yourself on what kind of relationship you desire. (First write it, then speak it.)

_____

_____

_____

_____

_____

_____

STEP 2: Request it in prayer. (First write it, then speak it.)

_____

_____

_____

_____

_____

_____

_____

STEP 3: Thank God for it as if it's already been done. (First write it, then speak it.)

_____

_____

_____

_____

_____

_____

_____

Loyal and faithful men do exist.

Today's Affirmation: _____

I am BLESSED with:

1. _____

2. _____

3. _____

4. _____

5. _____

MANIFEST THE MAN GOD HAS FOR YOU - DAILY PRACTICE

STEP 1: Get clear with yourself on what kind of relationship you desire. (First write it, then speak it.)

_____

_____

_____

_____

_____

_____

STEP 2: Request it in prayer. (First write it, then speak it.)

_____

_____

_____

_____

_____

_____

_____

_____

STEP 3: Thank God for it as if it's already been done. (First write it, then speak it.)

_____

_____

_____

_____

_____

_____

_____

_____

You can't keep entertaining the wrong man
expecting to receive the right one.

Today's Affirmation: _____

I am BLESSED with:

1. _____

2. _____

3. _____

4. _____

5. _____

MANIFEST THE MAN GOD HAS FOR YOU - DAILY PRACTICE

STEP 1: Get clear with yourself on what kind of relationship you desire. (First write it, then speak it.)

_____

_____

_____

_____

_____

_____

STEP 2: Request it in prayer. (First write it, then speak it.)

_____

_____

_____

_____

_____

_____

_____

STEP 3: Thank God for it as if it's already been done. (First write it, then speak it.)

_____

_____

_____

_____

_____

_____

_____

_____

The man God has for you wants to be the man you can count on, not the one who constantly lets you down.

Today's Affirmation: _____

I am BLESSED with:

1. _____

2. _____

3. _____

4. _____

5. _____

MANIFEST THE MAN GOD HAS FOR YOU - DAILY PRACTICE

STEP 1: Get clear with yourself on what kind of relationship you desire. (First write it, then speak it.)

_____

_____

_____

_____

_____

_____

STEP 2: Request it in prayer. (First write it, then speak it.)

_____

_____

_____

_____

_____

_____

_____

_____

STEP 3: Thank God for it as if it's already been done. (First write it, then speak it.)

_____

_____

_____

_____

_____

_____

_____

You deserve a man who loves you, respects you, and is attentive to your needs. Don't feel like you have to settle for anything less.

Today's Affirmation: _____

I am BLESSED with:

1. _____

2. _____

3. _____

4. _____

5. _____

MANIFEST THE MAN GOD HAS FOR YOU - DAILY PRACTICE

STEP 1: Get clear with yourself on what kind of relationship you desire. (First write it, then speak it.)

_____

_____

_____

_____

_____

STEP 2: Request it in prayer. (First write it, then speak it.)

_____

_____

_____

_____

_____

_____

_____

_____

STEP 3: Thank God for it as if it's already been done. (First write it, then speak it.)

_____

_____

_____

_____

_____

_____

_____

_____

Love is a beautiful thing. Embrace it.

Today's Affirmation: _____

I am BLESSED with:

1. _____

2. _____

3. _____

4. _____

5. _____

MANIFEST THE MAN GOD HAS FOR YOU - DAILY PRACTICE

STEP 1: Get clear with yourself on what kind of relationship you desire. (First write it, then speak it.)

_____

_____

_____

_____

_____

_____

STEP 2: Request it in prayer. (First write it, then speak it.)

_____

_____

_____

_____

_____

_____

_____

_____

STEP 3: Thank God for it as if it's already been done. (First write it, then speak it.)

_____

_____

_____

_____

_____

_____

_____

_____

Stop overthinking.
Don't stress yourself out.
Just let it go.

Today's Affirmation: _____

I am BLESSED with:

1. _____

2. _____

3. _____

4. _____

5. _____

MANIFEST THE MAN GOD HAS FOR YOU - DAILY PRACTICE

STEP 1: Get clear with yourself on what kind of relationship you desire. (First write it, then speak it.)

_____

_____

_____

_____

_____

STEP 2: Request it in prayer. (First write it, then speak it.)

_____

_____

_____

_____

_____

_____

_____

STEP 3: Thank God for it as if it's already been done. (First write it, then speak it.)

_____

_____

_____

_____

_____

_____

_____

The right man will give you things you never imagined.
Don't beg, he knows what you deserve.

Today's Affirmation: _____

I am BLESSED with:

1. _____

2. _____

3. _____

4. _____

5. _____

MANIFEST THE MAN GOD HAS FOR YOU - DAILY PRACTICE

STEP 1: Get clear with yourself on what kind of relationship you desire. (First write it, then speak it.)

_____

_____

_____

_____

_____

_____

STEP 2: Request it in prayer. (First write it, then speak it.)

_____

_____

_____

_____

_____

_____

_____

STEP 3: Thank God for it as if it's already been done. (First write it, then speak it.)

_____

_____

_____

_____

_____

_____

_____

Imagine a man praying to God that he gets to marry you.

Today's Affirmation: _____

I am BLESSED with:

1. _____

2. _____

3. _____

4. _____

5. _____

MANIFEST THE MAN GOD HAS FOR YOU - DAILY PRACTICE

STEP 1: Get clear with yourself on what kind of relationship you desire. (First write it, then speak it.)

_____

_____

_____

_____

_____

_____

STEP 2: Request it in prayer. (First write it, then speak it.)

_____

_____

_____

_____

_____

_____

_____

_____

STEP 3: Thank God for it as if it's already been done. (First write it, then speak it.)

_____

_____

_____

_____

_____

_____

_____

_____

When a man truly loves you, he wants to bring you clarity, not confusion.

Today's Affirmation: _____

I am BLESSED with:

1. _____

2. _____

3. _____

4. _____

5. _____

MANIFEST THE MAN GOD HAS FOR YOU - DAILY PRACTICE

STEP 1: Get clear with yourself on what kind of relationship you desire. (First write it, then speak it.)

_____

_____

_____

_____

_____

_____

STEP 2: Request it in prayer. (First write it, then speak it.)

_____

_____

_____

_____

_____

_____

_____

_____

STEP 3: Thank God for it as if it's already been done. (First write it, then speak it.)

_____

_____

_____

_____

_____

_____

_____

_____

Never regret being a good woman to the wrong man. His loss.

Today's Affirmation: _____

I am BLESSED with:

1. _____

2. _____

3. _____

4. _____

5. _____

MANIFEST THE MAN GOD HAS FOR YOU - DAILY PRACTICE

STEP 1: Get clear with yourself on what kind of relationship you desire. (First write it, then speak it.)

_____

_____

_____

_____

_____

_____

STEP 2: Request it in prayer. (First write it, then speak it.)

_____

_____

_____

_____

_____

_____

_____

_____

STEP 3: Thank God for it as if it's already been done. (First write it, then speak it.)

_____

_____

_____

_____

_____

_____

_____

_____

The man God Has for you will pull you closer to God, not further away from Him.

Today's Affirmation: _____

I am BLESSED with:

1. _____

2. _____

3. _____

4. _____

5. _____

MANIFEST THE MAN GOD HAS FOR YOU - DAILY PRACTICE

STEP 1: Get clear with yourself on what kind of relationship you desire. (First write it, then speak it.)

_____

_____

_____

_____

_____

_____

STEP 2: Request it in prayer. (First write it, then speak it.)

_____

_____

_____

_____

_____

_____

_____

_____

STEP 3: Thank God for it as if it's already been done. (First write it, then speak it.)

_____

_____

_____

_____

_____

_____

_____

_____

I pray you receive the man who wants to love you.

Today's Affirmation: _____

I am BLESSED with:

1. _____

2. _____

3. _____

4. _____

5. _____

MANIFEST THE MAN GOD HAS FOR YOU - DAILY PRACTICE

STEP 1: Get clear with yourself on what kind of relationship you desire. (First write it, then speak it.)

_____

_____

_____

_____

_____

_____

STEP 2: Request it in prayer. (First write it, then speak it.)

_____

_____

_____

_____

_____

_____

_____

_____

STEP 3: Thank God for it as if it's already been done. (First write it, then speak it.)

_____

_____

_____

_____

_____

_____

_____

_____

Some men will be lessons, some will be a waste of time, and one will be the man God has for you.

Today's Affirmation: _____

I am BLESSED with:

1. _____

2. _____

3. _____

4. _____

5. _____

MANIFEST THE MAN GOD HAS FOR YOU - DAILY PRACTICE

STEP 1: Get clear with yourself on what kind of relationship you desire. (First write it, then speak it.)

_____

_____

_____

_____

_____

_____

STEP 2: Request it in prayer. (First write it, then speak it.)

_____

_____

_____

_____

_____

_____

_____

_____

STEP 3: Thank God for it as if it's already been done. (First write it, then speak it.)

_____

_____

_____

_____

_____

_____

_____

_____

The wrong man will never be able to truly appreciate the good woman that you are.

Today's Affirmation: _____

I am BLESSED with:

1. _____

2. _____

3. _____

4. _____

5. _____

MANIFEST THE MAN GOD HAS FOR YOU - DAILY PRACTICE

STEP 1: Get clear with yourself on what kind of relationship you desire. (First write it, then speak it.)

_____

_____

_____

_____

_____

_____

STEP 2: Request it in prayer. (First write it, then speak it.)

_____

_____

_____

_____

_____

_____

_____

_____

STEP 3: Thank God for it as if it's already been done. (First write it, then speak it.)

_____

_____

_____

_____

_____

_____

_____

_____

His attention means nothing if you don't have his respect.

Today's Affirmation: _____

I am BLESSED with:

1. _____

2. _____

3. _____

4. _____

5. _____

MANIFEST THE MAN GOD HAS FOR YOU - DAILY PRACTICE

STEP 1: Get clear with yourself on what kind of relationship you desire. (First write it, then speak it.)

_____

_____

_____

_____

_____

_____

STEP 2: Request it in prayer. (First write it, then speak it.)

_____

_____

_____

_____

_____

_____

_____

_____

STEP 3: Thank God for it as if it's already been done. (First write it, then speak it.)

_____

_____

_____

_____

_____

_____

_____

Don't let the person who didn't embrace your value cause you to forget how valuable you really are.

Today's Affirmation: _____

I am BLESSED with:

1. _____

2. _____

3. _____

4. _____

5. _____

MANIFEST THE MAN GOD HAS FOR YOU - DAILY PRACTICE

STEP 1: Get clear with yourself on what kind of relationship you desire. (First write it, then speak it.)

_____

_____

_____

_____

_____

_____

STEP 2: Request it in prayer. (First write it, then speak it.)

_____

_____

_____

_____

_____

_____

_____

STEP 3: Thank God for it as if it's already been done. (First write it, then speak it.)

_____

_____

_____

_____

_____

_____

_____

_____

As a woman, your intuition is one of your greatest gifts. Don't ignore it, be willing to embrace it.

Today's Affirmation: _____

I am BLESSED with:

1. _____

2. _____

3. _____

4. _____

5. _____

MANIFEST THE MAN GOD HAS FOR YOU - DAILY PRACTICE

STEP 1: Get clear with yourself on what kind of relationship you desire. (First write it, then speak it.)

_____

_____

_____

_____

_____

_____

STEP 2: Request it in prayer. (First write it, then speak it.)

_____

_____

_____

_____

_____

_____

_____

_____

STEP 3: Thank God for it as if it's already been done. (First write it, then speak it.)

_____

_____

_____

_____

_____

_____

_____

_____

Queens don't chase. That's how your crown falls off.

Today's Affirmation: _____

I am BLESSED with:

1. _____

2. _____

3. _____

4. _____

5. _____

MANIFEST THE MAN GOD HAS FOR YOU - DAILY PRACTICE

STEP 1: Get clear with yourself on what kind of relationship you desire. (First write it, then speak it.)

_____

_____

_____

_____

_____

_____

STEP 2: Request it in prayer. (First write it, then speak it.)

_____

_____

_____

_____

_____

_____

_____

STEP 3: Thank God for it as if it's already been done. (First write it, then speak it.)

_____

_____

_____

_____

_____

_____

_____

_____

God is preparing your future husband. he's coming.

Today's Affirmation: _____

I am BLESSED with:

1. _____

2. _____

3. _____

4. _____

5. _____

MANIFEST THE MAN GOD HAS FOR YOU - DAILY PRACTICE

STEP 1: Get clear with yourself on what kind of relationship you desire. (First write it, then speak it.)

_____

_____

_____

_____

_____

_____

STEP 2: Request it in prayer. (First write it, then speak it.)

_____

_____

_____

_____

_____

_____

_____

STEP 3: Thank God for it as if it's already been done. (First write it, then speak it.)

_____

_____

_____

_____

_____

_____

_____

If he doesn't respect you, then he doesn't deserve you.

Today's Affirmation: _____

I am BLESSED with:

1. _____

2. _____

3. _____

4. _____

5. _____

MANIFEST THE MAN GOD HAS FOR YOU - DAILY PRACTICE

STEP 1: Get clear with yourself on what kind of relationship you desire. (First write it, then speak it.)

_____

_____

_____

_____

_____

_____

STEP 2: Request it in prayer. (First write it, then speak it.)

_____

_____

_____

_____

_____

_____

_____

_____

STEP 3: Thank God for it as if it's already been done. (First write it, then speak it.)

_____

_____

_____

_____

_____

_____

_____

_____

You deserve a man who makes you a priority, not a convenience.

Today's Affirmation: _____

I am BLESSED with:

1. _____

2. _____

3. _____

4. _____

5. _____

MANIFEST THE MAN GOD HAS FOR YOU - DAILY PRACTICE

STEP 1: Get clear with yourself on what kind of relationship you desire. (First write it, then speak it.)

_____

_____

_____

_____

_____

_____

STEP 2: Request it in prayer. (First write it, then speak it.)

_____

_____

_____

_____

_____

_____

_____

STEP 3: Thank God for it as if it's already been done. (First write it, then speak it.)

_____

_____

_____

_____

_____

_____

_____

Don't just ask God to send you a man, ask Him how to prepare and position you to receive the man He has for you.

Today's Affirmation: _____

I am BLESSED with:

1. _____

2. _____

3. _____

4. _____

5. _____

MANIFEST THE MAN GOD HAS FOR YOU - DAILY PRACTICE

STEP 1: Get clear with yourself on what kind of relationship you desire. (First write it, then speak it.)

_____

_____

_____

_____

_____

STEP 2: Request it in prayer. (First write it, then speak it.)

_____

_____

_____

_____

_____

_____

_____

STEP 3: Thank God for it as if it's already been done. (First write it, then speak it.)

_____

_____

_____

_____

_____

_____

_____

You are the woman a good man is praying for...

Today's Affirmation: _____

I am BLESSED with:

1. _____

2. _____

3. _____

4. _____

5. _____

MANIFEST THE MAN GOD HAS FOR YOU - DAILY PRACTICE

STEP 1: Get clear with yourself on what kind of relationship you desire. (First write it, then speak it.)

_____

_____

_____

_____

_____

_____

STEP 2: Request it in prayer. (First write it, then speak it.)

_____

_____

_____

_____

_____

_____

_____

_____

STEP 3: Thank God for it as if it's already been done. (First write it, then speak it.)

_____

_____

_____

_____

_____

_____

_____

_____

The same walls you have up to "protect" you,
are the same walls blocking your blessings.

Today's Affirmation: _____

I am BLESSED with:

1. _____

2. _____

3. _____

4. _____

5. _____

MANIFEST THE MAN GOD HAS FOR YOU - DAILY PRACTICE

STEP 1: Get clear with yourself on what kind of relationship you desire. (First write it, then speak it.)

_____

_____

_____

_____

_____

_____

STEP 2: Request it in prayer. (First write it, then speak it.)

_____

_____

_____

_____

_____

_____

_____

_____

STEP 3: Thank God for it as if it's already been done. (First write it, then speak it.)

_____

_____

_____

_____

_____

_____

_____

_____

You should never have to fight for or beg for their love. You deserve better than that.

Today's Affirmation: _____

I am BLESSED with:

1. _____

2. _____

3. _____

4. _____

5. _____

MANIFEST THE MAN GOD HAS FOR YOU - DAILY PRACTICE

STEP 1: Get clear with yourself on what kind of relationship you desire. (First write it, then speak it.)

_____

_____

_____

_____

_____

_____

STEP 2: Request it in prayer. (First write it, then speak it.)

_____

_____

_____

_____

_____

_____

_____

STEP 3: Thank God for it as if it's already been done. (First write it, then speak it.)

_____

_____

_____

_____

_____

_____

_____

_____

No man can heal you.
No man can make you whole.
You have to find your true self first.

Today's Affirmation: _____

I am BLESSED with:

1. _____

2. _____

3. _____

4. _____

5. _____

MANIFEST THE MAN GOD HAS FOR YOU - DAILY PRACTICE

STEP 1: Get clear with yourself on what kind of relationship you desire. (First write it, then speak it.)

_____

_____

_____

_____

_____

STEP 2: Request it in prayer. (First write it, then speak it.)

_____

_____

_____

_____

_____

_____

_____

_____

STEP 3: Thank God for it as if it's already been done. (First write it, then speak it.)

_____

_____

_____

_____

_____

_____

_____

_____

When a man truly loves you,
he wants to pray for you, not play games with you.

Today's Affirmation: _____

I am BLESSED with:

1. _____

2. _____

3. _____

4. _____

5. _____

MANIFEST THE MAN GOD HAS FOR YOU - DAILY PRACTICE

STEP 1: Get clear with yourself on what kind of relationship you desire. (First write it, then speak it.)

_____

_____

_____

_____

_____

_____

STEP 2: Request it in prayer. (First write it, then speak it.)

_____

_____

_____

_____

_____

_____

_____

_____

STEP 3: Thank God for it as if it's already been done. (First write it, then speak it.)

_____

_____

_____

_____

_____

_____

_____

_____

You are a great woman and you deserve a great love.

Today's Affirmation: _____

I am BLESSED with:

1. _____

2. _____

3. _____

4. _____

5. _____

MANIFEST THE MAN GOD HAS FOR YOU - DAILY PRACTICE

STEP 1: Get clear with yourself on what kind of relationship you desire. (First write it, then speak it.)

_____

_____

_____

_____

_____

_____

STEP 2: Request it in prayer. (First write it, then speak it.)

_____

_____

_____

_____

_____

_____

_____

STEP 3: Thank God for it as if it's already been done. (First write it, then speak it.)

_____

_____

_____

_____

_____

_____

_____

_____

If you keep giving yourself to a man who won't commit to you, how can you expect to receive a man who will.

Today's Affirmation: _____

I am BLESSED with:

1. _____

2. _____

3. _____

4. _____

5. _____

MANIFEST THE MAN GOD HAS FOR YOU - DAILY PRACTICE

STEP 1: Get clear with yourself on what kind of relationship you desire. (First write it, then speak it.)

_____

_____

_____

_____

_____

_____

STEP 2: Request it in prayer. (First write it, then speak it.)

_____

_____

_____

_____

_____

_____

_____

_____

STEP 3: Thank God for it as if it's already been done. (First write it, then speak it.)

_____

_____

_____

_____

_____

_____

_____

_____

Being single can be a great experience when you embrace it as an opportunity to heal and grow.

Today's Affirmation: _____

I am BLESSED with:

1. _____

2. _____

3. _____

4. _____

5. _____

MANIFEST THE MAN GOD HAS FOR YOU - DAILY PRACTICE

STEP 1: Get clear with yourself on what kind of relationship you desire. (First write it, then speak it.)

_____

_____

_____

_____

_____

_____

STEP 2: Request it in prayer. (First write it, then speak it.)

_____

_____

_____

_____

_____

_____

_____

STEP 3: Thank God for it as if it's already been done. (First write it, then speak it.)

_____

_____

_____

_____

_____

_____

_____

When a man loves you, he wants to bring you peace, not drama.

Today's Affirmation: _____

I am BLESSED with:

1. _____

2. _____

3. _____

4. _____

5. _____

MANIFEST THE MAN GOD HAS FOR YOU - DAILY PRACTICE

STEP 1: Get clear with yourself on what kind of relationship you desire. (First write it, then speak it.)

_____

_____

_____

_____

_____

_____

STEP 2: Request it in prayer. (First write it, then speak it.)

_____

_____

_____

_____

_____

_____

_____

STEP 3: Thank God for it as if it's already been done. (First write it, then speak it.)

_____

_____

_____

_____

_____

_____

_____

*Don't lean on your own understanding.
Ask God if the person you're with is truly best for you.*

Today's Affirmation: _____

I am BLESSED with:

1. _____

2. _____

3. _____

4. _____

5. _____

MANIFEST THE MAN GOD HAS FOR YOU - DAILY PRACTICE

STEP 1: Get clear with yourself on what kind of relationship you desire. (First write it, then speak it.)

_____

_____

_____

_____

_____

_____

STEP 2: Request it in prayer. (First write it, then speak it.)

_____

_____

_____

_____

_____

_____

_____

STEP 3: Thank God for it as if it's already been done. (First write it, then speak it.)

_____

_____

_____

_____

_____

_____

_____

_____

Don't give up on love.

Today's Affirmation: _____

I am BLESSED with:

1. _____

2. _____

3. _____

4. _____

5. _____

MANIFEST THE MAN GOD HAS FOR YOU - DAILY PRACTICE

STEP 1: Get clear with yourself on what kind of relationship you desire. (First write it, then speak it.)

_____

_____

_____

_____

_____

_____

STEP 2: Request it in prayer. (First write it, then speak it.)

_____

_____

_____

_____

_____

_____

_____

_____

STEP 3: Thank God for it as if it's already been done. (First write it, then speak it.)

_____

_____

_____

_____

_____

_____

_____

_____

We all fall, but we have to keep getting back up.

Today's Affirmation: _____

I am BLESSED with:

1. _____

2. _____

3. _____

4. _____

5. _____

MANIFEST THE MAN GOD HAS FOR YOU - DAILY PRACTICE

STEP 1: Get clear with yourself on what kind of relationship you desire. (First write it, then speak it.)

_____

_____

_____

_____

_____

_____

STEP 2: Request it in prayer. (First write it, then speak it.)

_____

_____

_____

_____

_____

_____

_____

STEP 3: Thank God for it as if it's already been done. (First write it, then speak it.)

_____

_____

_____

_____

_____

_____

_____

_____

*Don't allow negative people to rob you of your peace.
Take a deep breath and get back to being blessed.*

Today's Affirmation: _____

I am BLESSED with:

1. _____

2. _____

3. _____

4. _____

5. _____

MANIFEST THE MAN GOD HAS FOR YOU - DAILY PRACTICE

STEP 1: Get clear with yourself on what kind of relationship you desire. (First write it, then speak it.)

_____

_____

_____

_____

_____

_____

STEP 2: Request it in prayer. (First write it, then speak it.)

_____

_____

_____

_____

_____

_____

_____

_____

STEP 3: Thank God for it as if it's already been done. (First write it, then speak it.)

_____

_____

_____

_____

_____

_____

_____

_____

*Never forgot that you are a child of God,
and He only wants the best for you.*

Today's Affirmation: _____

I am BLESSED with:

1. _____

2. _____

3. _____

4. _____

5. _____

MANIFEST THE MAN GOD HAS FOR YOU - DAILY PRACTICE

STEP 1: Get clear with yourself on what kind of relationship you desire. (First write it, then speak it.)

_____

_____

_____

_____

_____

_____

STEP 2: Request it in prayer. (First write it, then speak it.)

_____

_____

_____

_____

_____

_____

_____

STEP 3: Thank God for it as if it's already been done. (First write it, then speak it.)

_____

_____

_____

_____

_____

_____

_____

Be patient, and only enter into a relationship when it is truly best for you.

Today's Affirmation: _____

I am BLESSED with:

1. _____

2. _____

3. _____

4. _____

5. _____

MANIFEST THE MAN GOD HAS FOR YOU - DAILY PRACTICE

STEP 1: Get clear with yourself on what kind of relationship you desire. (First write it, then speak it.)

_____

_____

_____

_____

_____

_____

STEP 2: Request it in prayer. (First write it, then speak it.)

_____

_____

_____

_____

_____

_____

_____

_____

STEP 3: Thank God for it as if it's already been done. (First write it, then speak it.)

_____

_____

_____

_____

_____

_____

_____

_____

Don't give up on getting what you deserve.

Today's Affirmation: _____

I am BLESSED with:

1. _____

2. _____

3. _____

4. _____

5. _____

MANIFEST THE MAN GOD HAS FOR YOU - DAILY PRACTICE

STEP 1: Get clear with yourself on what kind of relationship you desire. (First write it, then speak it.)

_____

_____

_____

_____

_____

_____

STEP 2: Request it in prayer. (First write it, then speak it.)

_____

_____

_____

_____

_____

_____

_____

_____

STEP 3: Thank God for it as if it's already been done. (First write it, then speak it.)

_____

_____

_____

_____

_____

_____

_____

_____

God did not forget about you. His timing is just different from yours. Stay positive and trust that everything is working for your good.

Today's Affirmation: _____

I am BLESSED with:

1. _____

2. _____

3. _____

4. _____

5. _____

MANIFEST THE MAN GOD HAS FOR YOU - DAILY PRACTICE

STEP 1: Get clear with yourself on what kind of relationship you desire. (First write it, then speak it.)

_____

_____

_____

_____

_____

STEP 2: Request it in prayer. (First write it, then speak it.)

_____

_____

_____

_____

_____

_____

_____

_____

STEP 3: Thank God for it as if it's already been done. (First write it, then speak it.)

_____

_____

_____

_____

_____

_____

_____

_____

Prayer is powerful.

Today's Affirmation: _____

I am BLESSED with:

1. _____

2. _____

3. _____

4. _____

5. _____

MANIFEST THE MAN GOD HAS FOR YOU - DAILY PRACTICE

STEP 1: Get clear with yourself on what kind of relationship you desire. (First write it, then speak it.)

_____

_____

_____

_____

_____

_____

STEP 2: Request it in prayer. (First write it, then speak it.)

_____

_____

_____

_____

_____

_____

_____

STEP 3: Thank God for it as if it's already been done. (First write it, then speak it.)

_____

_____

_____

_____

_____

_____

_____

_____

Be good to you.

Today's Affirmation: _____

I am BLESSED with:

1. _____

2. _____

3. _____

4. _____

5. _____

MANIFEST THE MAN GOD HAS FOR YOU - DAILY PRACTICE

STEP 1: Get clear with yourself on what kind of relationship you desire. (First write it, then speak it.)

_____

_____

_____

_____

_____

_____

STEP 2: Request it in prayer. (First write it, then speak it.)

_____

_____

_____

_____

_____

_____

_____

_____

STEP 3: Thank God for it as if it's already been done. (First write it, then speak it.)

_____

_____

_____

_____

_____

_____

_____

_____

Make room for the love you desire.

Today's Affirmation: _____

I am BLESSED with:

1. _____

2. _____

3. _____

4. _____

5. _____

MANIFEST THE MAN GOD HAS FOR YOU - DAILY PRACTICE

STEP 1: Get clear with yourself on what kind of relationship you desire. (First write it, then speak it.)

_____

_____

_____

_____

_____

_____

STEP 2: Request it in prayer. (First write it, then speak it.)

_____

_____

_____

_____

_____

_____

_____

_____

STEP 3: Thank God for it as if it's already been done. (First write it, then speak it.)

_____

_____

_____

_____

_____

_____

_____

*God is not only preparing you for him,
he is preparing him for you.*

Today's Affirmation: _____

I am BLESSED with:

1. _____

2. _____

3. _____

4. _____

5. _____

MANIFEST THE MAN GOD HAS FOR YOU - DAILY PRACTICE

STEP 1: Get clear with yourself on what kind of relationship you desire. (First write it, then speak it.)

_____

_____

_____

_____

_____

_____

STEP 2: Request it in prayer. (First write it, then speak it.)

_____

_____

_____

_____

_____

_____

_____

_____

STEP 3: Thank God for it as if it's already been done. (First write it, then speak it.)

_____

_____

_____

_____

_____

_____

_____

_____

The process may be hard to understand, but if God is leading you through it, then you're on the right track.

Today's Affirmation: _____

I am BLESSED with:

1. _____

2. _____

3. _____

4. _____

5. _____

MANIFEST THE MAN GOD HAS FOR YOU - DAILY PRACTICE

STEP 1: Get clear with yourself on what kind of relationship you desire. (First write it, then speak it.)

_____

_____

_____

_____

_____

_____

STEP 2: Request it in prayer. (First write it, then speak it.)

_____

_____

_____

_____

_____

_____

_____

STEP 3: Thank God for it as if it's already been done. (First write it, then speak it.)

_____

_____

_____

_____

_____

_____

_____

Believe in what you pray for.

Today's Affirmation: _____

I am BLESSED with:

1. _____

2. _____

3. _____

4. _____

5. _____

MANIFEST THE MAN GOD HAS FOR YOU - DAILY PRACTICE

STEP 1: Get clear with yourself on what kind of relationship you desire. (First write it, then speak it.)

_____

_____

_____

_____

_____

_____

STEP 2: Request it in prayer. (First write it, then speak it.)

_____

_____

_____

_____

_____

_____

_____

STEP 3: Thank God for it as if it's already been done. (First write it, then speak it.)

_____

_____

_____

_____

_____

_____

_____

Single and waiting is better than taken and faking.

Today's Affirmation: _____

I am BLESSED with:

1. _____

2. _____

3. _____

4. _____

5. _____

MANIFEST THE MAN GOD HAS FOR YOU - DAILY PRACTICE

STEP 1: Get clear with yourself on what kind of relationship you desire. (First write it, then speak it.)

_____

_____

_____

_____

_____

_____

STEP 2: Request it in prayer. (First write it, then speak it.)

_____

_____

_____

_____

_____

_____

_____

_____

STEP 3: Thank God for it as if it's already been done. (First write it, then speak it.)

_____

_____

_____

_____

_____

_____

_____

_____

Being single isn't a negative time in your life.
It's the time to get 100 percent happy with you.

Today's Affirmation: _____

I am BLESSED with:

1. _____

2. _____

3. _____

4. _____

5. _____

MANIFEST THE MAN GOD HAS FOR YOU - DAILY PRACTICE

STEP 1: Get clear with yourself on what kind of relationship you desire. (First write it, then speak it.)

_____

_____

_____

_____

_____

_____

STEP 2: Request it in prayer. (First write it, then speak it.)

_____

_____

_____

_____

_____

_____

_____

_____

STEP 3: Thank God for it as if it's already been done. (First write it, then speak it.)

_____

_____

_____

_____

_____

_____

_____

_____

You deserve peace, love, and happiness.

Today's Affirmation: _____

I am BLESSED with:

1. _____

2. _____

3. _____

4. _____

5. _____

MANIFEST THE MAN GOD HAS FOR YOU - DAILY PRACTICE

STEP 1: Get clear with yourself on what kind of relationship you desire. (First write it, then speak it.)

_____

_____

_____

_____

_____

_____

STEP 2: Request it in prayer. (First write it, then speak it.)

_____

_____

_____

_____

_____

_____

_____

_____

STEP 3: Thank God for it as if it's already been done. (First write it, then speak it.)

_____

_____

_____

_____

_____

_____

_____

_____

When one door closes, another one opens.

Today's Affirmation: _____

I am BLESSED with:

1. _____

2. _____

3. _____

4. _____

5. _____

MANIFEST THE MAN GOD HAS FOR YOU - DAILY PRACTICE

STEP 1: Get clear with yourself on what kind of relationship you desire. (First write it, then speak it.)

_____

_____

_____

_____

_____

_____

STEP 2: Request it in prayer. (First write it, then speak it.)

_____

_____

_____

_____

_____

_____

_____

_____

STEP 3: Thank God for it as if it's already been done. (First write it, then speak it.)

_____

_____

_____

_____

_____

_____

_____

_____

*More people should learn to be friends first
and stop rushing into relationships.*

Today's Affirmation: _____

I am BLESSED with:

1. _____

2. _____

3. _____

4. _____

5. _____

MANIFEST THE MAN GOD HAS FOR YOU - DAILY PRACTICE

STEP 1: Get clear with yourself on what kind of relationship you desire. (First write it, then speak it.)

_____

_____

_____

_____

_____

_____

STEP 2: Request it in prayer. (First write it, then speak it.)

_____

_____

_____

_____

_____

_____

_____

_____

STEP 3: Thank God for it as if it's already been done. (First write it, then speak it.)

_____

_____

_____

_____

_____

_____

_____

_____

May your character preach more loudly than your words.

Today's Affirmation: _____

I am BLESSED with:

1. _____

2. _____

3. _____

4. _____

5. _____

MANIFEST THE MAN GOD HAS FOR YOU - DAILY PRACTICE

STEP 1: Get clear with yourself on what kind of relationship you desire. (First write it, then speak it.)

_____

_____

_____

_____

_____

_____

STEP 2: Request it in prayer. (First write it, then speak it.)

_____

_____

_____

_____

_____

_____

_____

STEP 3: Thank God for it as if it's already been done. (First write it, then speak it.)

_____

_____

_____

_____

_____

_____

_____

Be thankful for closed doors, detours, and roadblocks. They protect you from paths and places not meant for you.

Today's Affirmation: _____

I am BLESSED with:

1. _____

2. _____

3. _____

4. _____

5. _____

MANIFEST THE MAN GOD HAS FOR YOU - DAILY PRACTICE

STEP 1: Get clear with yourself on what kind of relationship you desire. (First write it, then speak it.)

_____

_____

_____

_____

_____

_____

STEP 2: Request it in prayer. (First write it, then speak it.)

_____

_____

_____

_____

_____

_____

_____

_____

STEP 3: Thank God for it as if it's already been done. (First write it, then speak it.)

_____

_____

_____

_____

_____

_____

_____

Even the strongest women just need to be loved.

Today's Affirmation: _____

I am BLESSED with:

1. _____

2. _____

3. _____

4. _____

5. _____

MANIFEST THE MAN GOD HAS FOR YOU - DAILY PRACTICE

STEP 1: Get clear with yourself on what kind of relationship you desire. (First write it, then speak it.)

_____

_____

_____

_____

_____

_____

STEP 2: Request it in prayer. (First write it, then speak it.)

_____

_____

_____

_____

_____

_____

_____

_____

STEP 3: Thank God for it as if it's already been done. (First write it, then speak it.)

_____

_____

_____

_____

_____

_____

_____

_____

Let it go, give it to God, and prepare to receive something greater.

Today's Affirmation: _____

I am BLESSED with:

1. _____

2. _____

3. _____

4. _____

5. _____

MANIFEST THE MAN GOD HAS FOR YOU - DAILY PRACTICE

STEP 1: Get clear with yourself on what kind of relationship you desire. (First write it, then speak it.)

_____

_____

_____

_____

_____

_____

STEP 2: Request it in prayer. (First write it, then speak it.)

_____

_____

_____

_____

_____

_____

_____

_____

STEP 3: Thank God for it as if it's already been done. (First write it, then speak it.)

_____

_____

_____

_____

_____

_____

_____

_____

Worry and stress won't change anything.
Pray, relax, and trust God.

Today's Affirmation: _____

I am BLESSED with:

1. _____

2. _____

3. _____

4. _____

5. _____

MANIFEST THE MAN GOD HAS FOR YOU - DAILY PRACTICE

STEP 1: Get clear with yourself on what kind of relationship you desire. (First write it, then speak it.)

_____

_____

_____

_____

_____

_____

STEP 2: Request it in prayer. (First write it, then speak it.)

_____

_____

_____

_____

_____

_____

_____

STEP 3: Thank God for it as if it's already been done. (First write it, then speak it.)

_____

_____

_____

_____

_____

_____

_____

_____

Sometimes the grass looks greener on the other side, because the grass is fake.

Today's Affirmation: _____

I am BLESSED with:

1. _____

2. _____

3. _____

4. _____

5. _____

MANIFEST THE MAN GOD HAS FOR YOU - DAILY PRACTICE

STEP 1: Get clear with yourself on what kind of relationship you desire. (First write it, then speak it.)

_____

_____

_____

_____

_____

_____

STEP 2: Request it in prayer. (First write it, then speak it.)

_____

_____

_____

_____

_____

_____

_____

STEP 3: Thank God for it as if it's already been done. (First write it, then speak it.)

_____

_____

_____

_____

_____

_____

_____

When God blocks it, leave it alone.

Today's Affirmation: _____

I am BLESSED with:

1. _____

2. _____

3. _____

4. _____

5. _____

MANIFEST THE MAN GOD HAS FOR YOU - DAILY PRACTICE

STEP 1: Get clear with yourself on what kind of relationship you desire. (First write it, then speak it.)

_____

_____

_____

_____

_____

_____

STEP 2: Request it in prayer. (First write it, then speak it.)

_____

_____

_____

_____

_____

_____

_____

_____

STEP 3: Thank God for it as if it's already been done. (First write it, then speak it.)

_____

_____

_____

_____

_____

_____

_____

_____

Remember to pray for your friends and family. They may be dealing with a lot more than you know.

Today's Affirmation: _____

I am BLESSED with:

1. _____

2. _____

3. _____

4. _____

5. _____

MANIFEST THE MAN GOD HAS FOR YOU - DAILY PRACTICE

STEP 1: Get clear with yourself on what kind of relationship you desire. (First write it, then speak it.)

_____

_____

_____

_____

_____

_____

STEP 2: Request it in prayer. (First write it, then speak it.)

_____

_____

_____

_____

_____

_____

_____

STEP 3: Thank God for it as if it's already been done. (First write it, then speak it.)

_____

_____

_____

_____

_____

_____

_____

What is coming is better than what is gone.

Today's Affirmation: _____

I am BLESSED with:

1. _____

2. _____

3. _____

4. _____

5. _____

MANIFEST THE MAN GOD HAS FOR YOU - DAILY PRACTICE

STEP 1: Get clear with yourself on what kind of relationship you desire. (First write it, then speak it.)

_____

_____

_____

_____

_____

_____

STEP 2: Request it in prayer. (First write it, then speak it.)

_____

_____

_____

_____

_____

_____

_____

STEP 3: Thank God for it as if it's already been done. (First write it, then speak it.)

_____

_____

_____

_____

_____

_____

_____

Even when you're frustrated ... trust God.

Today's Affirmation: _____

I am BLESSED with:

1. _____

2. _____

3. _____

4. _____

5. _____

MANIFEST THE MAN GOD HAS FOR YOU - DAILY PRACTICE

STEP 1: Get clear with yourself on what kind of relationship you desire. (First write it, then speak it.)

_____

_____

_____

_____

_____

_____

STEP 2: Request it in prayer. (First write it, then speak it.)

_____

_____

_____

_____

_____

_____

_____

STEP 3: Thank God for it as if it's already been done. (First write it, then speak it.)

_____

_____

_____

_____

_____

_____

_____

Find God. Find You. Find Peace.

Today's Affirmation: _____

I am BLESSED with:

1. _____

2. _____

3. _____

4. _____

5. _____

MANIFEST THE MAN GOD HAS FOR YOU - DAILY PRACTICE

STEP 1: Get clear with yourself on what kind of relationship you desire. (First write it, then speak it.)

_____

_____

_____

_____

_____

_____

STEP 2: Request it in prayer. (First write it, then speak it.)

_____

_____

_____

_____

_____

_____

_____

_____

STEP 3: Thank God for it as if it's already been done. (First write it, then speak it.)

_____

_____

_____

_____

_____

_____

_____

_____

About the Author

Stephan Labossiere is *the* "Relationship Guy." An authority on real love, real talk, real relationships. The brand Stephan Speaks is synonymous with happier relationships and healthier people around the globe. For more than a decade, Stephan has committed himself to breaking down relationship barriers, pushing past common facades, and exposing the truth. It is his understanding of REAL relationships that has empowered millions of people, clients and readers alike, to create their best lives by being able to experience and sustain greater love.

Seen, heard, and chronicled in national and international media outlets including; the *Tom Joyner Morning Show, The Examiner, ABC,* GQ, and *Huffington Post Live.* The certified life & relationship coach, speaker, and award winning, bestselling author is the voice that the world tunes into for answers to their difficult relationship woes. From understanding the opposite sex, to navigating the paths and avoiding the pitfalls of relationships and self-growth, Stephan's relationship advice and insight helps countless men and women overcome the situations hindering them from achieving an authentically amazing life.

Stephan is highly sought-after because he is able to dispel the myths of relationship breakdowns and obstacles–platonic, romantic, and otherwise—with fervor and finesse. His signature style, relatability, and passion make international audiences sit up and pay attention.

"My message is simple: life and relationships require truth. The willingness to speak truth and the bravery to acknowledge truth is paramount."

Are you listening?

Enough said.

by Stephan Speaks

COMING SOON

Healing Heartbreak Journal
Love After Heartbreak, Vol. 1 Companion Book
www.HealingHeartbreakBook.com

JUST RELEASED

Love After Heartbreak, Vol. 1
www.LoveAfterHeartbreak.com

He's Lying Sis
www.HesLyingSis.com

Prayers For My Marriage
www.PrayersForMyMarriageBook.com

POPULAR BOOKS

The Man God Has for You
www.TheManGodHasForMe.com

God Where is My Boaz?
www.GodWhereIsMyBoaz.com

He Who Finds a Wife
www.HeWhoFinds.com

How to Get a Man to Cherish You if Your His Wife
www.GetAManToCherishYou.com

*How to Get a Woman to Have Sex With You
if Your Her Husband*
www.BetterMarriageBetterLoving.com